IMAGES
of England

TRANMERE ROVERS
FOOTBALL CLUB

Prenton Park as it is today, a superb all-seater stadium for almost 17,000 fans. What would the cricketers of Belmont and Lyndurst, who got together to form a football club in a ditch close to the site of the current ground 114 years ago, make of their creation now?

IMAGES
of England

TRANMERE ROVERS
FOOTBALL CLUB

Compiled by
Peter Bishop

TEMPUS

Tempus Publishing Limited
The Mill, Brimscombe Port,
Stroud, Gloucestershire, GL5 2QG

ISBN 0 7524 1505 0

Typesetting and origination by
Tempus Publishing Limited
Printed in Great Britain by
Midway Colour Print, Wiltshire

Present and forthcoming football titles in the *Archive Photograph Series*:

Bristol Rovers
Burnley
Bury
Cardiff City 1899-1947
Cardiff City 1947-1971
Charlton Athletic
Crewe Alexandra
Crystal Palace
Exeter City
Gillingham
Luton Town
Newport County 1912-1960
Oxford United
Plymouth Argyle 1886-1986
Reading
Sheffield United
Sunderland
Swansea Town 1912-1986
Tranmere Rovers
Wrexham
York City

Contents

Foreword

If the BBC ever get round to producing a *Mastermind* special for football fans, the author of this excellent pictorial history is a cert to sit on the black leather chair – 'Specialist subject Tranmere Rovers…your time starts now' – and Peter Bishop has got all manner of photographic evidence to back-up his in-depth knowledge. This book is a must for Rovers fans. It charts the history of a club that radiates warmth and generates smiles; the photographs capture the flow of the club down the years and the words add detail, to tell so many varied stories. The word 'crisis' is sure to appear a couple of times, but where would a family club like Tranmere be without a crisis or two…or three! And then there are the characters – hundreds of players, administrators and supporters have played their part in making Tranmere into one of the most popular clubs in English football. Through words and pictures, Peter's book gives you the facts and captures the humour: I met so many old friends going through this book and team photographs bring back so many great memories. Anyway, time and space is running out here (and in *Mastermind* you can't afford any misplaced passes), so here goes…name the American goalkeeping dentist who conducted Rovers board meetings by transatlantic conference call? Who scored Rovers' winner in the 1973 League Cup tie at Highbury? Did Johnny King ever bake that cake? Have you ever seen a better goalscorer than Aldo? All these answers are in the book, but for the record: Bruce Osterman, Eddie Loyden, yes, and no (but George Yardley was very, very good). This is a great book about a great football club.

Ray Stubbs

Introduction

My old history teacher, Harry Pugh, would never have thought it possible. At the age of fifteen, I neither knew nor cared why the Crimean War started. Yet here I am, some thirty years later, penning the introduction for my second Tranmere book, labelled by some as 'The Club Historian'!

It must be said that history as taught in state schools during the 1960s was less than inspiring – I ask you, why would anybody need to know the exact date Napoleon was banished to Elba? However, when it comes to delving into the history of something that matters to you, now that, as they say, is a whole different ball game. Some people become fascinated by their family roots; others turn their attention to collecting memorabilia of some sort. Both activities represent an interest in history, however tenuous. Indeed, historical research is something one tends to drift into subconsciously without appreciating how difficult you will find it to extricate yourself from the web of intrigue. One uncovered item of interest tends to encourage a further dip into the archives and so on....

When I became the programme editor for Tranmere Rovers in 1984, I had no ambition or desire to trace the history of the club; even less writing books on it, but my postbag changed all that. Fans wanted to know about personalities and games from the past, articles needed to be garnished with photographs. Enquiries at the club established no records existed, while the entire photograph collection consisted of eight team photographs from the 'sixties and 'seventies on the wall of an executive lounge. Enter one of my regular correspondents, Gilbert Upton, a Tranmere fanatic who I had initially branded a nuisance because he had (rightly) taken me to task over inaccuracies in my seasonal statistics! Gil had just bought himself a computer, but had no purpose for it in mind. On the other hand, I had a problem locating and storing information. The perfect partnership was born as we realised that if we pooled our resources and efforts we could amass a vast amount of information by systematically checking the microfilm copies of every *Birkenhead News* in the library, from 1881 onwards. Thus started the marathon task of discovering and re-writing the club's history and acquiring the photograph collection that forms the backbone of this book.

The delight one feels when an old picture, which has lain unseen in someone's loft for over half a century, comes to light is immense, as each one represents another piece of the jigsaw. However, there have been moments of despair, like the time a firm of commercial photographers told us they had destroyed their entire collection of post-war Tranmere photographs and negatives a few months before I contacted them.

From thirteen years of research have come five books, including this one, and possibly scope for more. My own *A-Z Of Tranmere Rovers*, published in 1990, is now the 'J.R. Hartley' category, while Gil has most recently published *A Complete Record* with Steve Wilson, to add to his two previous works on the history of the club between 1881 and 1921, and the life and times of Dixie Dean whilst at Tranmere.

While one is conscious the production of such club histories is very much a modern phenomenon, with the advent of computer databases, it is still amazing that not one volume on the club's past had been published before 1990. Now, for the first time, Tranmere's long, and often fascinating, past has been portrayed pictorially and I am very proud to be able to say I was the one asked to compile it.

Having kept and catalogued all the worthwhile photographs commissioned by the club since 1984 and set myself the task of finding (and copying where necessary) as many old team, action and news photos as I could trace, the collection from which the selection in this book is drawn has now grown to around 1,000 pictures. There are, of course, gaps and to anyone who thinks they or their forefathers should have been featured but who are absent, I apologise. In some cases I just do not have a particular photograph, or the picture quality is less than is demanded in the production of this book.

During the acquisition of the photograph collection and the compilation of this book, I have been helped by many people and I would now like to place on record my sincere thanks, starting firstly with Gil – for his help, friendship and encouragement over the years – and then the former chairman, Mr Frank Corfe, for his support and permission to use club photographs of events since 1987 to supplement my own private collection.

The vast bulk of the pre-war photographs were copied from the collection of Sydney Rogers, who inherited them via a friend who was carrying out a house clearance at the former home of the ex-secretary/manager Bert Cooke – thank God they did not end up on the tip! Tranmere Rovers certainly owe Syd a debt of thanks for keeping them safe until I could copy them.

The *Liverpool Echo*, via their sports editor, Ken Rogers, have been a great help, providing access to their photographic library to enable me to fill in the gaps in our collection. My sincere thanks also to club photographers Bob and Frazer Bird, George Jenkinson, Paul Beecham and Peter Fardoe; former players Harold Atkinson, Ralph Millington, the late 'Bunny' Bell and Ray Mathias for access to their own collections and the many others who have contributed individual photos to the cause.

Hopefully, the photographs and text in this book will evoke many memories for all followers of Tranmere Rovers. Having been one myself for around thirty years, it has been both a pleasure and an honour to be involved with the club and this project. Finally, it has to be said that were it not for my wonderful wife, Maria, it would not have been possible. Infinitely patient, she understood why I had to hide myself away for a few months to complete this book, which I dedicate to our children Kate and Mark, my father John and late mother, Kathleen.

It is a fact of life everyone hopes to make some sort of impression on his or her chosen profession or interest and leave a legacy to be remembered by.

Maybe Harry Pugh did make his mark on that fifteen-year-old after all…

Peter Bishop
September 1998

8

One
Non-League Days: 1885-1921

The earliest known picture of Tranmere Rovers, taken in 1889/90, featuring many of the players who were founder members. Note how the players had been positioned to follow the profile of the hedge! From left to right, back row: Myers (Secretary), J.H. McGaul (President), Munro, Morgan (Captain), H. Sheridan, Shepherd, F. Rogers, Jackson, Wild. Middle row: Wallace. Front row (seated): Roberts, G. Sheridan, Littler, E. Rogers, McAfee.

Centre half 'Joe' Robson (in the middle, wearing the white shirt) was one of Tranmere's most loyal players in the early days, playing from around 1891 until 1910. This particular photograph was taken in 1905, in front of the dressing rooms at the old Prenton Park which is the site of Temple Road School today.

Though this picture was taken at the start of the 1907/08 season, it was later overprinted with the title 'Combination Champions' after Rovers claimed top spot, on goal average, from second-placed Chester. Dick Ledsome (far right) was the club's first 'manager'.

The earliest known action photograph of Rovers, taken on 24 January 1914 when they played Wallasey Borough in the Wirral Senior Cup Final. In the background, the Borough Road side is still uncovered.

Pictured during his term as Mayor of Birkenhead in 1908, Alderman James Hannay McGaul JP, was a founder member and president until the club became a limited company in 1912. He died in 1921, having achieved his lifetime's ambition of seeing Rovers in the Football League.

In 1913/14, Rovers were champions of the Lancashire Combination, a feat built upon the goal scoring of Stan Rowlands and Reg Leck, who are pictured together in the middle of the front row. From left to right, back row: Hancock, Robinson, -?-, Ashcroft, -?-. Front row: Moreton, Cunningham, Rowlands, Leck, Gould, -?-.

Johnny Campbell played for Rovers, at right-back, from 1914 to 1929 but never became a professional, preferring to retain his amateur status. Despite the handicap of a bullet embedded in his skull, he lived to the grand age of eighty-seven and it was his proud boast never to have been cautioned or sent off.

The caption describes Reg Leck's goal against Fleetwood at Prenton Park on 10 April 1914 as 'clever'. It may well have been, but what about the goalkeeper's headgear?

Stan Rowlands closes in on South Liverpool 'keeper Bradshaw, as fans look on from the Borough Road side – then referred to as the 'Popular' side. The roof didn't go on until Rovers were set for the Football League in 1920.

By 1912, Rovers had moved across Prenton Road West from the Borough Road Enclosure to their current ground and had a flourishing reserve side. From left to right, back row: Hill, Robinson, Rimmer, Parkin, Darlington, Scholes, Simms. Front row: B. Cooke, Loughlin, Smith, Hunter, Leck, Osborne.

Stan Rowlands was the first Rovers player to win a full international cap when he played for Wales *v.* England in 1913/14. During that season, his thirty-two goals helped the club win the Lancashire Combination Championship.

On 29 November 1913, Tranmere thrashed South Liverpool 7-0 at Prenton Park. Charlie Cunningham smashes the ball past 'keeper Bradshaw for one of the goals. Crowds at this time averaged 5,000.

Rovers line up for the camera at the end of 1913/14 season, with the Lancashire Combination Championship Trophy (centre) and two others won by the reserves – one being the Birkenhead Hospitals Cup.

The First World War is over and Tranmere are back to winning ways, pictured here in May 1919 with the Cheshire Senior Cup and the Lancashire Combination Trophy – the fruits of the 1918/19 season. The Combination Trophy was presented on 21 April while the Cheshire Senior Cup was won thanks to a 6-0 victory over Altrincham five days later. The photograph also features Alfred H. Mayor, who became secretary shortly after the club was formed. From left to right, back row: H. Roberts, G. Dimmer, Bull, Wilde, Simpson, T. Hill, F. Jones. Middle row: B. Cooke, G.H. Hall, Smith, Scott, Hilton, Campbell, P. Powell, F. Jones. Front row: J. Tart, Cunningham, Owen, Thomas, Leck, Gaskell (Trainer), A.H. Mayor, R. Ledsom. Sitting cross-legged: Moreton, Latta.

The Rovers team that played in the Central League in 1919. From left to right, back row: Cooke, Cunningham, Sugden, Bradshaw, Campbell, Leddy, Stuart. Front row: Moreton, Leck, Williamson, Fairclough, Roberts, Gaskill

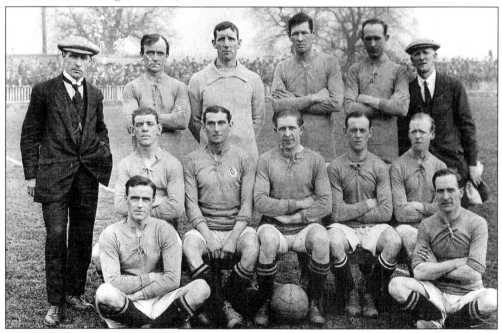

On the back row of this 1919/20 team shot, stands Joe Mercer Snr, father of the Everton, Arsenal and, later, City and England boss, Joe. From left to right, back row: Cooke, Ellis, McDonald, Mercer, Stuart, Gaskill (Trainer). Middle row: Cunningham, Groves, Wright, Leck, Bunting. Front row: Moreton, Tattum.

The two men who shaped Tranmere between 1910 and 1935. On the left, Jimmy Moreton was a player and, later, a trainer, until he died in 1942. Secretary/manager Bert Cooke, on the right, was a wheeler and dealer, selling players such as Dixie Dean and Pongo Waring – who he introduced to League football. This photograph was taken in 1921.

'Pa' McGaul's dream is finally realised. The players line up before Rovers first-ever Football League match, against Crewe, on 27 August 1921. For the record they were, from left to right, back row: Cooke, Campbell, Milnes, Heslop, Bradshaw, Stuart, Grainger, Gaskill. Front row: Moreton, Groves, Hyam, Ford, Hughes

Two
Shooting Stars:
1921-1945

During the roaring 'twenties and 'thirties, many of the great names in the game cut their football teeth at Prenton Park – and were quickly sold on to other beneficiaries. This shot shows the greatest of them all, seventeen-year-old William Ralph 'Dixie' Dean, in the 1924/25 line-up (holding the ball).

The Rovers squad for their first-ever season in the Football League in 1921/22. With crowds around the 6,000 mark and money tight, the club made little impact in its early years – save its ability to discover a succession of 'shooting stars'. Over the next twenty years there would be only occasional flirtations with success.

Tommy Stuart was Rovers' regular left-back between 1921 and 1927, when he made 205 appearances and scored thirteen goals. Signed from Bootle Albion, he was to become one of the stalwarts of the early League years, even though it is said he lacked the athleticism of his contemporaries.

Tranmere's squad for 1922/23 season, pictured in front of the old dressing rooms on the corner of Borough Road and Prenton Road West. Second left on the back row is George Moorhouse, who later emigrated to the USA and played for them in two World Cups!

George Moorhouse – the first Englishman to play in the World Cup. A player with Rovers between 1921 and 1923, he packed his bags and headed for the 'Big Apple' and later appeared for the USA in two World Cups in 1930 and 1934 after becoming an American citizen (photograph courtesy of the US National Soccer Hall of Fame).

In 1922, Rovers' goalkeeper was Harry Bradshaw (centre, back row) who had been signed from South Liverpool a year earlier where he had regularly played against Rovers. Bradshaw was, at five feet and seven inches, probably the smallest Tranmere 'keeper ever, but was regarded as one of the bravest.

In 1923, Tranmere signed a fast, clever centre forward from Millwall named Stan Sayer. He scored thirty-three goals in eighty-seven matches, but more importantly became the mentor and tutor of young Dixie Dean. Here, Sayer is pictured in a match against New Brighton in October 1923.

By 1923, Frank Mitchell, a big Scotsman signed from Liverpool, had replaced the diminutive Harry Bradshaw between the sticks. Here, Mitchell is pictured saving from Nevin of Barrow in a 3-0 victory on 22 September 1923.

Stan Sayer was nothing if not brave. Both he and New Brighton 'keeper, Mehaffy, were injured in this clash at Prenton Park on 13 October 1923. Such was the crowd, 15,416, that many fans sat on the touchline in front of the Borough Road enclosure. Unfortunately, Rovers lost 2-1!

Grimsby Town left Prenton Park pointless on the opening day of the 1923/24 season, thanks to this winning goal from Stan Sayer, which delighted the 8,000 crowd.

Arthur Briggs took over the goalkeeper's shirt from Frank Mitchell in 1924 and kept it for eight years, during which time he made 246 appearances. Signed from Hull City, he was virtually an ever-present for several seasons.

They used to say Stan Sayer enjoyed a pint in the Prenton before the game, however it never seemed to affect his ability to jump and head a ball. As young Dixie learned his trade, it was Sayer who took him under his wing.

Centre half Vince Matthews joined Rovers from Bolton in 1925 and never missed a match until he was transferred to Sheffield United for £1,000 in 1927. Whilst with the Blades, he went onto play for England against France and Belgium at the end of 1927/28 season. Born in Aylesbury, he returned to Buckinghamshire when his career finished, and he died in 1950. A cultured attacking centre half, he was well ahead of his time.

Can you imagine a player today being pictured with sticking plasters on his face? This 1925/26 team shot shows Norman Proctor had been in the wars. From left to right, back row: Jackson, Leslie, Briggs, Thirkell, Smith. Front row: White, Littlehales, Marquis, Proctor, Chalmers, Matthews.

Safe under the watchful eye of 'the long arm of the law', Rovers won the Cheshire Senior Cup at Northwich Victoria's ground in 1926 and George Jackson, the captain, lifted the trophy. The Cheshire Senior Cup was also won in the seasons 1920/21, 1927/28 and 1931/32.

The team, which featured a mixture of reserve and first-team players, line up with the Cheshire Senior Cup at Northwich in 1926. From left to right (players only), back row: Barton, Johnson, Burrows, Smith, Naylor. Front row: T.J. Jones, White, Fogg, G. Jackson, Littlehales, Roberts, Rimmer

Ellis Rimmer was a brilliant fleet-footed winger, who made only sixty-one League appearances (scoring twenty goals) before being transferred to Sheffield Wednesday in 1928. At Hillsborough, he won League and FA Cup honours as well as four England caps. Another player in the long line of Tranmere's gifts to the wider game, Ellis died in 1965, having returned home to Birkenhead to run a public house. His nephew, Warwick Rimmer, continues the family connection with Rovers as the club's highly-rated youth development officer.

In the 1920s, few players seemed to last longer than a couple of seasons. This 1926/27 line-up would be the last for many of these players. From left to right, back row: Cooke, Marquis, Yates, Briggs, Thirkell, Matthews, Lewis. Front row: Moreton, Charlton, Evans, Hogan, Cartman.

In 1927, a youngster with the wonderful nickname of 'Pongo' (his real name was Tom) Waring came into the side, having previously been on the groundstaff and a seller of cigarettes to the crowd! Waring became one of the game's great centre forwards and signalled his arrival with twenty-four goals – including a (then) club record six against Durham City – in his first twenty-seven League matches. However, he soon went the way of many others and was sold to Aston Villa, on 17 February 1928, for £4,700. Here 'Pongo' is pictured in his England shirt before one of his five full international appearances.

Inseparable pals and playing partners, Ellis Rimmer and Tommy Jones, are pictured side-by-side on this 1926/27 team photograph. From left to right, back row: Yates, Barton, Briggs, Matthews, Thirkell, Cooke, Lewis. Front row: White, Proctor, Flanagan, Jones, Rimmer, Evans

Tommy Jones served Rovers both as a player and, later, as a trainer. Another Welshman from mid-Rhondda, Jones partnered Ellis Rimmer at inside left, until the latter left for Sheffield Wednesday in 1928, and then followed him to Hillsborough to renew their successful left-wing combination. The holder of two Welsh caps in 1931/32, Tommy later played for Manchester United and Watford before having a spell between 1946 and 1953 as trainer back at Tranmere.

In an era when having action or still photographs to accompany lengthy match reports was almost unheard of, Glover's cartoons were a regular feature in the Birkenhead News. This one was published around September 1927.

The 1928/29 squad of the first team and reserves, line up in front of the old dressing rooms. In the middle row, third from the left, is Bill Ridding. 'Nibbler' was another promising forward, but was sold, for a four-figure fee, to Manchester City. During the Second World War, Bill was trainer and manager at Rovers. He later became the boss at Bolton and took them to the 1953 FA Cup Final.

They used to enjoy a bit of horseplay, even back in 1928! Jack 'Ginger' Lewis, a Welshman from the Rhondda, played 288 times for Rovers between 1923 and 1934 and was famed for once singing in Woodside Station after returning home from a 7-3 victory at Darlington.

Tranmere Rovers, 1928/29 squad. From left to right, back row: Barton, A. Jackson, Moreton, G. Jackson, Briggs, Thirkell, Lewis. Front row: Jones, Charlton, Beswick, Littlehales, Cartman.

In the 1930/31 season, the inside forward partnership that Jack Kennedy (pictured) formed with Fred 'Farewell' Watts and Ernie Dixon produced a staggering ninety-three League goals! This remains a Football League record for three inside forwards (inside right, centre forward, inside left...in old money!). For the record, Kennedy got thirty-five, Dixon thirty-one and Watts twenty-seven.

Meet the directors – just prior to the 1931/32 season. From left to right: Cooke, Livingstone, Lewis, Meston, Dale, Lewins, Whitehurst (at back), Barton, Gray, Adams, Urmson, Moreton (Trainer), Littlehales (in front), Spencer, Cook, Watts, Dixon, Briggs (at back), Kennedy, Fishwick.

Fag in hand, the club's chairman, Lt Col. W.H. Stott, welcomes the players at the start of 1930/31 season. From left to right, back row: Kennedy, Watts, Briggs, Littlehales, Meston, Adams, Shears, Moore. Front row: Lt Col. Stott, Urmson, J. Kennedy, Moreton, Murphy, Livingstone, Cooke

During the 1932/33 season, Rovers celebrated their jubilee – incorrectly – with a glittering dinner at Birkenhead Town Hall for officials of the FA and Football League, plus local dignitaries. We now know the jubilee celebrations should have taken place in 1935.

In May 1935, Rovers won the Welsh Cup for the first and only time, beating Chester 1-0. This photo was taken with the trophy before the start of the following season. As captain at the time, it was Bert Gray (in the centre, at the back) who lifted the cup.

On Boxing Day 1935, Robert 'Bunny' Bell created a bit of football history when he scored nine goals in the 13-4 defeat of Oldham. Bell, pictured (left) with Teddy Barton, held the Football League record for just four months, but is still Rovers' top scorer in any match.

On 13 March 1936, Everton signed Bunny Bell from Tranmere as cover for Tommy Lawton, in exchange for Archie Clark, who became captain of our championship side two years later. The Everton boss, Theo Kelly, stands over Bell while Jim Knowles watches Clark in the lounge of the Vines Hotel.

The hero returns to his roots – 'Pongo' Waring, with his mother, outside the family home in Church Road, Tranmere, on 18 October 1936: this was the day he rejoined Tranmere Rovers. Then a thirty-year-old international player of some standing, Pongo would lead Rovers to the Third Division (North) title in 1937/38. Don't you just love the plus fours!

For the first time in forty years, Rovers had a separate manager and secretary in 1936/37. From left to right, back row: Knowles (Secretary), R. Spencer, Platt, McLaren, Gray, Amery, Bradshaw, Carr (Manager), Hurrell (Director). Front row: Eden, Donald, Crompton, Woodward, Urmson

The Tranmere team that won the Division Three (North) championship in 1937/38. From left to right, back row: Knowles (Secretary/Manager), King, Spencer, Hamilton, Curnow, Wassell, Anderson, Clark (Captain). Front row: Dellow, Davis, Waring, Eden, Cassidy.

Rovers' squad for the big adventure of the 1938/39 season – their first-ever in Division Two. From left to right, back row: Knowles, Moore, Moreton, Trueman, Perfect, Davies, Kearns, Walton, Curnow, Lewis, Griffiths, Walkden, Owen, Cassidy, Mason, McDonald, Rawcliffe, Jackson. Middle row: Fletcher (Chairman), Waring, Anderson, Eden, Day, Hamilton, Clark, Wassell, Thomas, Smith, Docking, Dr French. Front row: Gaskell, Jones, Flowers, Obrey, Dellow, Buckley, Spencer, Aldiss, Kearney, Jackson.

Workmen attempt to repair the back of the Borough Road side, after it was damaged during the Second World War when a landmine dropped onto one of the new houses opposite.

Three
The Great Underachievers: 1945-1962

All aboard the charabanc! Rovers fans are up for the cup in February 1952, as they set off from Haymarket in Birkenhead for Huddersfield – and what a day they had, Tranmere winning the game 2-1. Not a replica team shirt in sight though…

The Berlin airlift is underway, Prince Charles is born and many foodstuffs are still rationed – meanwhile, the Rovers class of 1948 looks forward to a new season.

The Tranmere team pictured at Haig Avenue, Southport, just before the start of 1949/50 season. From left to right, back row: Wheeler, Steele, Lloyd, Bell, Williams, McDonald. Front row: Harlock, Bainbridge, Atkinson, Eastham, Wood.

Abe Rosenthal was a rotund but hugely popular forward who flitted between Tranmere and Bradford City four times because he had an ice cream business there! A very skilful player, Abe, pictured here in October 1950 at Prenton Park, scored forty-four goals in his 130 games for the club.

Prenton Park in 1948, viewed from the corner of the old main stand and the cowshed. Note the old scoreboard on top of the Kop and the uncovered Borough Road side – the roof having been removed as unsafe.

It's November 1950 and Rovers are playing a local derby with Chester. George Payne, Rovers 'keeper, punches clear to deny Hankinson, Burgess and Devonshire of Chester, as Harold Bell, Len Keiran (6) and Lol Hodgson (3) look on.

A case of the usual suspects again! Those lining up for the camera, prior to the match with Southport on 12 March 1949, were, from left to right, back row: Bainbridge, Bell, Lloyd, Keiran, McBennett. Front row: Eastham, Steele, Connor, Wheeler, Aldiss, Atkinson

George Greens' superb cartoon tells the story of Tranmere's 8-1 thrashing of Ashington in the FA Cup First Round on 22 November 1952. Harold Atkinson scored six to set a new FA Cup record, which he held until 1972, when Ted McDougall netted nine at Margate.

Bill Bainbridge (8) hitches a ride on the back of an Oldham defender as the Latics' 'keeper, Ogden, attempts a clearance in the match held on 19 February 1951. Note all the buses lined up on Borough Road.

Billy Gibson, Lloyd Iceton and Len Keiran enjoy a spot of 'head tennis' in front of the old main stand prior to the big FA Cup tie with Spurs in January 1953, which Rovers drew 1-1, with a goal from Iceton.

It's pre-season 1952/53, and the squad line up behind the dressing rooms at the rear of the Kop. From left to right, back row: R. Williams, Keiran, Cartwright, Eastham, G. Payne, Lloyd, Done, H. Bell, Mycock, Gibson. Middle row: Dillon, Davies, Lamb, A. Payne, Iceton, Bainbridge, Williamson, Steele. Front row: Harlock, Jackson, Hodgson, Atkinson.

In 1951/52, it took Rovers four matches and 402 minutes to overcome non-League Blyth Spartans. This team group, which features Abe Rosenthal (on the front row), who scored four times in the tie, was taken before the first match on 15 December 1951 at Prenton Park: the game ended 1-1.

Players, Officials Of Tranmere Rovers

HAROLD BELL

LLOYD ICETON

COUN. J. H. HODGKINSON (CHAIRMAN)

KEN McDEVITT

'RAY' DAVIES

HAROLD LLOYD

RALPH MILLINGTON

'BILL' BAINBRIDGE

PERCY STEELE

'BILL' GIBSON

H. ATKINSON

'LEN' KIERAN

JACK JONES

'STEW' WILLIAMSON

SEC. MR. E. BLACKBURN

Cartoons by 'Gwil' were a feature of the *Liverpool Evening Express* in the early 1950s. This collection of Tranmere faces was published prior to Rovers' Fourth Round FA Cup tie at Chelsea, which ended in a 4-0 thrashing in front of 59,000 plus fans. In the corner, Ernie Blackburn, a man rarely photographed, is given the 'Gwil' treatment. Director Bill Bothwell said of Blackburn, several years later, 'He always made a penny do the work of a shilling'.

The original cowshed had a five-span roof and was erected in the 1931/32 season at a cost of £1,000. Much of the steelwork did indeed come from a farm – hence the nickname. Though this view was taken in 1954, the town end remained unchanged until gale damage in 1973 necessitated its demolition and replacement with a three-span structure.

A rare photograph of Tranmere in their black and white change strip of the 1954/55 season. From left to right, back row: Jones, Millington, Bell, Lloyd, Keiran, Lamont, Rimmer. Front row: McDevitt, Atkinson, Done, Walls, Woan

Holding the ball in this 1954 team photograph is Cyril Done, who bludgeoned his way to seventy-five goals in ninety-seven games, including fourteen in the FA Cup. Brilliant in the air, he was signed from Liverpool in May 1952.

TRANMERE ROVERS F.C.

By 1955/56, Ernie Blackburn had stepped down from the dual secretary/manager role allowing Noel Kelly (pictured front row, second left) to take over as player/manager – the club's first such appointment.

A crowd of 6,000 turned up to see Rovers take on Liverpool Reserves in the Liverpool Senior Cup Semi-final in April 1956. Percy Steele and Ralph Millington close in on Bimpson of Liverpool as Harold Bell watches.

Let there be light! A crowd of 16,728 pack Prenton Park on 29 September 1958 to witness the switching on of Rovers' first set of floodlights, paid for with a £15,000 donation from the Supporters' Association. The picture shows Ralph Millington in aerial combat in the game, which was against Rochdale.

The 1958/59 team, assembled by player/manager Peter Farrell. From left to right, back row: Woodruff (Coach), Millington, Rowley, Bell, Payne, Dodd, Heydon, Charlton. Front row: McDonnell, K. Williams, Eglington, Farrell, McDevitt, Frith.

Irish international winger Tommy Eglington – a huge pal of Peter Farrell's – joined Rovers in June 1957, so it was no surprise when Farrell crossed the Mersey from Everton four months later. A brilliant goalscoring winger, he netted forty goals in 181 outings before returning home to Dublin in 1962. Tommy played twenty-four times for Eire and six times for Northern Ireland. Simply known as 'Eggo', he was a huge crowd favourite.

Harold Bell holds the all-time record for the most consecutive League appearances. Between 1946 and 1955 he never missed a match, playing 401 games. Indeed, if you add on FA Cup, Liverpool Senior Cup and Cheshire Bowl matches, the run extends to 459 games! Bell joined Rovers in 1939 and finally retired in 1960, having been the ultimate one-club man – a true sportsman and gentleman. In total, he made 595 League appearances (a club record), although Ray Mathias has played more games including cup ties.

Chairman, Alderman Hugh Platt, and the vice-chairman, Ted Wright (extreme left), shake hands with, captain, Ralph Millington in August 1960, while Peter Farrell introduces new signings Willie Sinclair (ex-Huddersfield) and Stan Billington (ex-Everton). In the background, the secretary, Peter Graves, looks on. Farrell however, was sacked on 12 December, as Rovers tumbled towards Division Four.

This is how I want you to play this season! Peter Farrell, back in training kit, talks tactics to Keith Williams, Bobby Harrop, Ralph Millington, Gordon Clayton, George Payne and David Frith, just prior to the start of the 1960/61 season.

Tony Rowley lobs George Payne during a pre-season Tranmere *v.* Liverpool fixture in 1957. Rowley later joined Tranmere and became a full Welsh international with Rovers, netting forty-nine goals in 109 games – a bargain for £3,500.

In August 1960, Peter Farrell signed a Nigerian student who was studying at Birkenhead Technical College. He proved an instant sensation, but faded later on. Elkanah Onyeali – or 'Al' as the fans called him – was the first black player at Prenton Park. This cartoon, by 'Vern', reflects his popularity at the time.

Elkanah Onyeali may only have been a part-timer, due to his studies, but the twenty-two-year-old Nigerian international centre forward still managed to get himself onto this 1960/61 team photograph. From left to right, back row: Billington, Millington, Payne, McDonnell, Best, Eglington. Front row: Finney, Barnett, Frith, Mulkerrin, Onyeali.

Four

The Russell Era
and Beyond:
1962-1980

It's January 1963, there's snow on the ground, and Rovers are due to face Chelsea at Prenton Park in the FA Cup! The frozen souls in the new, all-white kit, introduced by Russell, were, from left to right, back row: Jackie Wright (Trainer), J. King, Neil, Conroy, Leyland, Wilson, Frith, Dave Russell (Manager). Front row: Campbell, Jones, Hickson, Gubbins, Finney.

The big freeze of 1963 put football on hold for several weeks. In an attempt to make Prenton Park playable, Rovers recruited the services of an Eastham farmer, Mr W. Davies, and his tractor, before the match with Darlington. Also pictured are the groundsman, Stan Matthews, and manager, Dave Russell. For the record, the match was postponed!

At Prenton Park in 1965, this was the squad who were pacemakers in Division Four for most of the season. From left to right, back row: Stanley, Lornie, Hill, Pritchard, Leyland, Robertson, A'Court, A. King, Martin, Halliday. Front row: Twist, Parnell, Sinclair, Dyson, J. King, Stuart, Manning, Conde, Richardson.

A trip to Morecambe was Dave Russell's prescription to pep up the squad in February 1965, as they tried to get in shape for the promotion push. From the top of the ladder: Alan King, A'Court, John King, Robertson, Dyson, Leyland, Manning, McDonnell, Sinclair and Mandy Hill.

It's July 1965, and the cameras pop into Prenton Park to see the players under starter's orders for the new season. Joey Pritchard, 'Sancho' Parnell and Harry Leyland lead the way.

The loss of John Manning for several of the 1964/65 run-in matches proved disastrous to promotion hopes, with the 4-2 home defeat by Oxford on 17 April proving the hammer blow. In Manning's absence, John Lornie moved up front and he is pictured heading past Oxford's Shuker, as Sinclair looks on.

Mr Chris Hodgson became Tranmere's chairman in October 1967. Here he is, pictured outside the old club offices in Prenton Road West. Hodgson remained at the helm until 1972. He was chairman and secretary of the Birkenhead Co-operative Society.

Rovers' old main stand, demolished in 1968, was an amalgamation of two separate stands. The centre portion was brought across the road from the old Prenton Park site, while the two wings were purchased in 1914 from Lever Bros, who were erecting a new stand at The Oval sports ground.

At the rear of the old wooden main stand at Prenton Park, there stood a single-storey building, which served the dual purpose of a supporters' canteen and a gym. Here, Chris Hodgson, the new chairman, is pictured walking between canteen and stand with his wife in October 1967.

Full-back Stan Storton avoids this challenge from a Barnsley defender to cross the ball during the 3-3 draw on 24 April 1967. Pictured in the background is the old main stand and paddock.

Given the passage of time, no one knows why Mr and Mrs Monty Lea were pictured, but this photograph does provide a splendid 1967 view of Rovers' old club offices at 14 Prenton Road West, which is now the Pizzaria Venezia. The boardroom was upstairs with the secretaries' offices downstairs.

George Yardley, a Prenton Park hero, puts Barnsley players under pressure in the 3-3 draw in April 1967. He scored fifteen league goals in the 1966/67 promotion campaign.

Champagne corks are popping! 'We've done it at last' was the message as Tranmere players celebrated promotion following a 3-1 victory over Rochdale on 12 May 1967. After narrowly missing out in the previous two seasons – one paper described it as a promotion push that had lasted 137 League games – Rovers enjoyed the moment and the vice-chairman, Bill Bothwell, looks happy too!

Chairman Fred Lloyd welcomes Johnny King, the club's captain, back to pre-season training in July 1967, as vice-chairman Bill Bothwell, manager Dave Russell and the squad look on. Lloyd resigned in September of that year, through ill-health.

January 1968 saw Huddersfield Town the visitors in the FA Cup. Here, the Town 'keeper, Oldfield, saves from Beamish as Mielezarek looks on.

Kenny Beamish scores Tranmere's first goal against Huddersfield Town in the FA Cup Third Round, 27 January 1968.

There are only a few minutes of the tie left and the score stands at 1-1 (Worthington having equalised), when little Graham Williams cuts in from the left and unleashes a twenty-five yard right-footer, which had Oldfield beaten all ends up. Rovers won 2-1.

64

In the Fourth Round of the FA Cup in 1967/68, Tranmere forced a draw at Coventry City and brought them back to Prenton Park, knowing victory would earn them a trip to Goodison. George Hudson is pictured here, scoring the first against City.

Almost 21,000 fans went crazy when George Yardley made it 2-0. As his partner, George Hudson, tries to congratulate him, a youngster jumps on his back in the mayhem – Everton here we come!

It's the build up to the Fifth Round tie at Everton in 1968, and players are persuaded to take up all manner of poses for the photographers. From left to right: MacNamee, Stevens, Yardley, Hudson, Williams and Hill. Sadly, Yardley would be seriously injured at Shrewsbury and he missed the big game.

Yet another photograph from before the clash with Everton, taken at The Oval. From left to right, back row: Robertson, Hill, MacNamee, A. King, Pritchard. Middle row: Yardley, Martin, Casey, Cumbes, Storton, Beamish, Wright (Trainer). Front row: Stevens, J. King, D. Russell (Manager), Williams, Hudson.

No sooner had this 1967/68 team photograph been taken, when Brian Clough whisked young centre half Roy McFarland (third from right, back row) off to Derby County for a mere £25,000. He would go on to play twenty-eight times for England. The transfer angered many Tranmere fans.

The late Lord Howell, then Sports Minister Dennis Howell, officially opens Rovers' new £80,000 main stand, on 20 December 1968. Watching are: Chris Hodgson (Rovers' chairman) and the Mayor of Birkenhead.

The Rovers squad, pictured in February 1968. From left to right, back row: Casey, Storton, Martin, Cumbes, A. King, Pritchard, J. King, J. Wright (Trainer). Front row: Beamish, Hudson, Stevens, Yardley, MacNamee.

In July 1969, Dave Russell decided to change normal pre-season routines and organised a spot of commando-style training up Moel Famau (554m) in North Wales, in order to get the team in shape.

Prenton Park saw its record attendance on 5 February 1972, when Stoke City faced Rovers in the FA Cup Fourth Round. Two down early on, Ron Yeats cracked a goal past Gordon Banks to send most of the 24,424 fans wild.

Two minutes from time, Kenny Beamish (8) equalised to give Rovers a deserved replay and spark off a pitch invasion and unbridled celebrations amongst the record crowd.

'Don't look at the camera' seems to be the maxim in this line-up before the 1972/73 season.
From left to right, back row: Crossley, D'arcy, Lawrence, Flood, Mathias, Molyneux, M. Moore.
Front row: Loyden, Sinclair, Veitch, Young, R. Yeats (Player/Manager).

Boxing Day 1972, and a crowd of 14,356 pack Prenton Park to see a 1-1 draw with Bolton
Wanderers. This view of the ground was taken from the top of the Kop, looking towards the
Main Stand and the five-span Cowshed.

This is one of the most famous goals, both in the history of Tranmere Rovers and indeed the League Cup, for it gave us a 1-0 victory at Arsenal on 2 October 1973. Unfortunately, the scorer of the goal, Eddie Loyden, is hidden behind Simpson and McNab of Arsenal, while Bob Wilson is grounded. It was one of the shock cup results of the decade.

It's July 1974 and the squad line up for the annual pre-season ritual with some new faces – including 6'6" goalkeeper David Johnson and a young Liverpool University student named Steve Coppell (far left, second row from the front), who would make a name for himself. Yeats, however, didn't last the season: he was sacked in April.

With Tranmere bottom of Division Three in November 1974, Ron Yeats called in his old Liverpool boss, Bill Shankly, as a 'consultant' and the legend quickly weaved his magic in the dressing room, inspiring three successive victories. Perhaps the best story concerning Shanks' time at Prenton Park took place while watching a reserve game. Asking about the rather static winger, Yeats said 'Oh, he's the PFA Union Rep boss', only for Shanks to snap 'Really? So why are you playing him when he's on strike'!

The 1975/76 squad that John King steered to promotion at the first time of asking. From left to right, back row: Evans, Hughes, Mercer, Stubbs, Chamborious, Postlewhite. Middle row: J. King, Russell, Griffiths, Philpotts, Moore, Johnson, Parry, Palios, Flood, Kenny, E. Robertson. Front row: Allen, Mitchell, Peplow, Mathias, Tynan, Young.

Captain, Ray Mathias, and top scorer, Ronnie Moore, lead the celebrations in the directors' box as fans on the pitch enjoy that 'promotion feeling', following a 3-3 home draw with Bradford City on 26 April 1976.

One of Rovers' longest-serving employees (as player, coach and member of the groundstaff), Ted Anderson, is pictured with, from left to right: Tommy Young, Tommy Veitch, Ronnie Moore and Bobby Tynan, in 1977. Moore scored thirty-four League goals in the 1975/76 promotion campaign.

From the start of the 1977/78 season until the 17 January, John King fielded the same eleven in thirty-two matches – twenty-eight of them in the League. For the record, the team that went unchanged for so long was: Dick Johnson, Ray Mathias, Eddie Flood, Les Parry, Dave Philpotts, Clive Evans, Steve Peplow, Mark Palios, Ronnie Moore, Bobby Tynan and Russ Allen. When Bobby Tynan got injured, however, John King was forced to change the line-up and bring in John James on 20 January.

The class of 1978/79 – which included BBC Sports presenter Ray Stubbs – were playing to ever-decreasing gates. From left to right, back row: D. Russell, Eaton, Kerr, Bramhall, Parry, Johnson, West, Moore, Tynan, Philpotts, Postlewhite, Stubbs, E. Robertson. Front row: Flood, Allen, Evans, J. King, Cliff, James, Peplow.

After seventeen years on the board, including several as vice-chairman, popular broadcaster and sports journalist, Bill Bothwell became the chairman of Rovers in 1972 and remained at the helm until 1980. He died, aged sixty-eight, the following year. A hugely popular figure in the football world, he would always bang the drum for Tranmere at any event and was a great innovator of fundraising ideas.

Tranmere Rovers' most famous hooligan! In 1979, a seventy-two-year-old pensioner, Charlie Lindsay, was arrested after he vented his frustration at Rovers' poor showing in a 5-0 home defeat by Bournemouth, by whacking the visiting 'keeper, Kenny Allen, across the backside with his walking stick as he prepared to take a goal kick.

In August 1978, winger Hughie McAuley – who had played on loan at Rovers previously – was signed by John King from Charlton Athletic for a (then) club record £20,000. The two are pictured outside the main entrance. It turned out to be a less than spectacular success and later that year McAuley was swapped for Carlisle's Jim Lumby.

Five

The Fall and Rise: 1980-1988

The dawn of the 1980s, and Rovers return to their all-white kit, albeit with a blue diagonal sash and socks. In September 1980, John King's first spell as manager was unceremoniously ended in the wake of relegation to Division Four and pitiful attendances.

Clive Evans – famed for his likeness to film star John Travolta – scores one of his two goals in a 5-1 drubbing of Rochdale in January 1980. It was a sign of the public apathy in Birkenhead that just 1,890 people watched the game, despite the traditional Friday night kick-off.

Gary Plumley of Newport County is injured by the challenge from Kenny Beamish in a 2-0 defeat by the Welshmen in February 1980. Newport's first goal – a penalty – was scored by John Aldridge.

With a side composed of pros, part-timers and apprentices, Tranmere were heading for trouble and eventual re-election in 1981, at the end of Bryan Hamilton's first season in charge. From left to right, back row: Mathias (Coach), Craven, Mountfield, Johnson, Endersby, Kelly, Kerr, Robertson (Assistant Manager). Front row: Powell, Mungall, Parry, Hamilton (Player/Manger), Mooney, Bramhall, Griffiths.

Bryan Hamilton's one piece of silverware during his tenure at Prenton Park – the Rovers players celebrate winning the Cheshire FA Premier Cup at Chester. Standing next to Bryan Hamilton is the assistant manager, Eddie Robertson, who tragically collapsed and died on West Kirby beach during a training session in December 1981.

With crowds hovering around the 1000 to 1200 mark, and the Wirral public apparently disinterested, Rovers were approaching their lowest ebb. Here, the paltry crowd watches Bobby Hutchinson and John Bramhall giving the Bournemouth defence a few problems.

John Kerr cracks in one of his two goals during a 2-2 draw with Sheffield United in March 1982, which attracted a large-for-the-time crowd of 4,675. However, the cash windfall was wiped out by damage to seating in the main stand caused by fights involving the Yorkshire club's travelling fans.

Welsh youth international Neville Powell cracks in a shot against Chesterfield in the League Trophy – a pre-season competition in August 1982.

There were smiles for this 1982 team shot, but there were soon a lot of worried faces in November, when Chairman Gerry Gould announced the club was bankrupt and would close inside a fortnight – following the collapse of a take-over bid by Birkenhead-born American tycoon Billy McAtteer.

Even though Rovers were incorrectly celebrating their centenary year, the sparsely-populated terraces reflect Tranmere's problems in 1982. No fans, no money, no saleable assets and half the ground closed for safety reasons. Here, 'Biffo' Griffiths and John Kerr try to get the better of Stockport in the 1-1 draw in September.

PLEASE MAKE A DONATION to the "SAVE ROVERS FUND" by going into ANY Bank and quoting the following: "SAVE ROVERS FUND" — National Westminster Bank, Charing Cross, Grange Road West, Birkenhead. (Branch Number: 600507), Account Number: 05029562, or, send your donation of cash or cheques to: "SAVE ROVERS FUND", C/O C.T. Young & Co., Chartered Accountants, 33 Oxton Road, Birkenhead, L41 2QQ. *Please give your name and address on all credit slips.*

SAVE ROVERS FUND

The fall, when it came, was not unexpected to those close to the club, but was greeted with a good deal of surprise, sympathy and goodwill elsewhere. Under the gaze of the TV documentary film-makers from the *Forty Minutes* programme, Rovers fans rallied around the club and formed a fighting fund, distributing leaflets (pictured alongside) around the town to help swell the club's coffers. The wider world of football also stepped in with money-spinning friendly ties against Wolves, Manchester United and Liverpool. Even a group of Watford fans sent a cheque for £400. The upshot was that enough money was raised to buy some time and Rovers were indeed saved when the local Council loaned them £200,000.

Wolves, who had been the first to offer help in November, returned to Prenton Park in January 1983, when fate decreed Rovers should meet them in the FA Cup Third Round, to give a further boost to the bank balance. Here, John Kerr tries to force his way past Palmer, but to no avail as Rovers lost 1-0.

General manager Jack Butterfield used to say 'we should pack in the football and just run the celebrity dinners'! Here, in September 1983, Stan Mortensen is entertaining diners. Steve Coppell is to his left. Held in the Vice-President Lounge, Tranmere's famed monthly celebrity dinners did indeed help keep the club afloat.

Bryan Hamilton takes his troops to a local gym for a good workout in 1983. Pictured toning his leg muscles up is Welsh international 'keeper Dai Davies, along with other members of the squad.

In 1984, Howard Kendall brought Everton over (as well as the newly-won FA Cup) for Ray Mathias' Testimonial Match. Ray holds the club record for the most career appearances, with 637 between 1967 and 1985. A 5,176 crowd turned out to mark his twenty-one years as a Tranmere player.

In July 1984, a San Franciscan lawyer and self-confessed soccer nut, Bruce Osterman, bought the club with promises of 'doing a Watford'. Osterman liked nothing more than to train with the players and perfect his goalkeeping technique, but this led to a showdown with boss Bryan Hamilton, in which there was only going to be one winner. He eventually sold his shareholding in 1987, after running up debts of £575,000 which led to an administration order under the 1986 Insolvency Act being invoked to prevent him winding up the company and selling the land.

The Hugh Foulerton Cutlery Player of the Month Award is handed to ace marksman John Clayton by Steve Edwards (right) in October 1984. Clayton and Colin Clarke scored sixty-five League and cup goals between them in 1984/85 – Clayton grabbing thirty-six.

John Aspinall, seen here scoring from the spot, was one of a number of local players recruited by Rovers on a part-time basis. Despite working a thirty-eight hour week as an electrician for BNFL, Aspinall played 139 times in two spells (between 1982-1984 and in 1987), scoring thirty goals.

Imagine turning down your chance of fame just to see Tranmere play Scunthorpe at home on a Friday night? Well, quirky Birkenhead rock band 'Half Man, Half Biscuit' did in 1986, turning down a appearance on Channel 4's *The Tube* because they wouldn't miss the match! The band also did a benefit concert for Rovers funds.

'We're crap but we can all balance the ball on the back of our necks!' – the Frank Worthington era lasted from July 1985 to March 1987. From left to right, back row: Sinclair, Ashcroft, Hilditch, Anderson. Middle row: Philpotts, Hollifield, Clayton, Atkins, Grierson, Miller, Worthington, Mulhall. Front row: Train, Muir, Edwards, Burgess, Mungall, Rodaway, Birch.

Mark Palios was a fully-qualified chartered accountant who was also a useful footballer and, like Aspinall and others, successfully maintained two separate careers with 278 appearances (with thirty-three goals) in two spells for the club. Here, Mark scores in the Freight Rover Trophy win over Blackpool in 1985.

It's April 1985 and John Aspinall's superb volley gives Southend 'keeper Jim Stannard no chance to bring warm applause from the two hundred souls on the Kop. Osterman's dreams were crumbling, as just 1,082 paid to watch this match.

On the fiftieth anniversary of his feat, Rovers invited Robert 'Bunny' Bell back to Prenton Park, along with his grandson Richard Caddy, to be presented with an inscribed silver salver and his old, long-lost match ball, marking his nine-goal haul in the record defeat of Oldham on 26 December 1935. Frank Worthington did the honours before the Burnley game.

The 1986/87 squad before the start of the season. By February, manager Frank Worthington and his staff were all long gone. From left to right, back row: Garnett, Thorpe, Hughes, McManus, Grierson, Moore, Vickers, Hay. Front row: Morrissey, Anderson, Bullock, Mungall, Bell, Muir.

The rescue party, pictured on 20 March 1987, following the takeover by the Peter Johnson/Frank Corfe regime. From left to right: Tony Adams (Director), Dr Mike Azurdia (Club Doctor), George Higham (Director), Peter Johnson, Frank Corfe, Frank Taylor (Administrator), John Holsgrove (Director).

John King returned to Tranmere as manager in April 1987, for a second spell at the helm. Here he is, being welcomed by the chief executive, Frank Corfe. Ronnie Moore, who had been manager for two months after Worthington was dismissed, became the first-team coach.

Probably the most important goal in Tranmere's history! At the end of 1986/87 season, Rovers had to win to preserve their League status and Gary William's late goal against Exeter sent an (official) crowd of 6,983 wild with delight.

In 1988, Tranmere qualified for the Mercantile Credit Football League Centenary Festival at Wembley – their first-ever visit to the twin towers. During the build-up to the big weekend, Tranmere fans came down with a variety of banners, knowing they were due to face Wimbledon in the opening game.

While many questioned the sense in cancelling a whole weekend's League programme for a meaningless tournament, over 3,000 Tranmere fans travelled to Wembley, determined to make it the party to end all parties and packing one end of a largely-deserted stadium.

Dave Martindale is mobbed beneath a pile of ecstatic Tranmere players after scoring against Wimbledon in the festival's opening game. Tranmere fans gained particular pleasure from the fact the side they defeated over twenty minutes managed to overturn Liverpool over ninety, six weeks later.

Ian Muir slots a penalty past Newcastle 'keeper Kelly to clinch Rovers' 2-0 victory in the twenty-minute match. John Morrissey had opened the scoring.

The final whistle of the Newcastle match goes and the whole squad whoop it up on Wembley's famous turf, milking the applause from all sides of the ground, which now had around 40,000 fans inside. A problem though, someone had to wash the white kit for Sundays' semi-final encounter with Forest, as they'd only brought one set of each with them!

A picture that really requires no caption as the giant Wembley scoreboard tells a story hardly any Tranmere fan can take in.

Such was the excitement of the club photographer (and avid fan), George Jenkinson, he completely lost his composure after Ian Muir scored against Nottingham Forest – hence the lop-sided view of Wembley and Ian's jig of delight!

A goal that made Brian Clough angry! Having scored a glorious opener, Ian Muir stole in at the far post to net another, but Forest hit back and we lost the subsequent penalty shoot-out decider. However, the glory of the whole weekend was Tranmere's alone.

'When I grow up I want to play for Tranmere, then England, and become a £1 million player'. Little boys' dreams do come true, but only if your name is Ian Moore and your dad is the Tranmere coach, Ronnie. Father and son are pictured in 1987.

The traditional pre-Wembley song was cut in a Bolton recording studio, and even included the voice of coach driver Colin Dyson! *Wembley Way* was written by the Supporters' Club secretary, Allen Price and also featured the vocals of singer Linda Christiansen. It didn't make the Top Twenty!

On 24 September 1987, the club celebrated the refurbishment of the Vice-President's Lounge by holding a 'Night of Nostalgia' for over fifty former players from different generations. Pictured here, from left to right, are: Charlie McDonnell, Alan King, George Yardley, Ralph Millington and Gerry Casey.

Six
A Journey to the Moon: 1988-1998

Having warned we may have created a monster (of expectancy) following the success at Wembley, John King was forced to mix his metaphors as the team mounted a promotion challenge in 1988/89. With the likes of John Morrissey and Ian Muir on fire, King (pictured) told the Wirral public to 'Come and join us on a journey to the moon...'!

Let there be light! The club's new £72,000 floodlights were officially switched on by League President Philip Carter at the start of 1988/89 season. Apart from Messrs Johnson and Corfe, Jim Pinnington of contractors James Heaney & Sons breathes a sigh of relief.

The glory days continued to roll and roll during 1988. In October, Mark Hughes scored the winner against Division One Middlesborough to dump them out of the League Cup. Steve Vickers and 8,000 delighted fans share 'Yozzers' magic moment.

In the next round of the League Cup, Blackpool were despatched, thanks to this great downward header from Eddie Bishop, to put Rovers into the last sixteen.

The squad which took Rovers back to Division Three in 1988/89. From left to right, back row: McKenna, Williams, Collings, Nixon, Higgins, Murray. Middle row: Jones (Trainer), Moore (Coach), Hughes, Steel, Vickers, Malkin, W. Rimmer (Youth Development Officer), N. Wilson (Secretary). Front row: Garnett, Morrissey, Martindale, McCarrick, J. King (Manager), Muir, Harvey, Mungall, Bishop.

They called it 'Friday Night Fever' when Tranmere played Scunthorpe in a vital promotion tussle in April 1988. Almost 10,500 were there to see John Morrissey (pictured) score in a 2-1 victory. The promised land was now in sight.

While Rovers were up at Hartlepool in April 1989, ninety-six Liverpool fans tragically died at Hillsborough. The following week, Prenton Park was the setting for a Memorial Service with Rovers and Liverpool skippers Jimmy Harvey and Ronnie Whelan leading the floral tributes. For once the red, blue and white of Merseyside were united in grief.

Above: Ian Muir's flicked header gave Tranmere the lead against fellow promotion hopefuls Crewe in May 1989. Though Crewe equalised and held on for a 1-1 draw, it was sufficient to clinch promotion for both clubs and many of the 15,286 crowd poured onto the pitch in joint celebration. *Below*: Mark McCarrick milks the applause from the directors' box.

With promotion in the bag, the annual Player of the Year bash took on an extra dimension. Award winners Ian Muir and Steve Mungall seem to be enjoying themselves.

'Going up, going up, going up!' For the first time in twelve years, the traditional song of success booms out from the Tranmere dressing-room in the wake of the final match of the 1988/89 season against Crewe. In the foreground is the Midlands League Championship Trophy, which had been won by the reserves.

Though not the most graceful of players, midfielder Eddie Bishop was hugely popular with fans. A man of many talents, Eddie was an accomplished portrait artist and is pictured above with Mohamed Ali and Liz Taylor. He was also no mean impersonator of Elvis and at a testimonial function for Steve Mungall, Eddie sang dozens of Elvis numbers to an enthralled audience. *Below*: Eddie goes through his routine for his team-mates.

The pride of Wirral. The Mayor and Mayoress of Wirral entertain the team, officials and directors at Birkenhead Town Hall, to honour promotion to Division Three and present the club with an engraved glass bowl to mark the occasion in December 1989.

Cementing the relationship! Chief executive Frank Corfe signs a sponsorship deal, which puts the name of 'Wirral' on Tranmere shirts, club stationary and publications. Present at this occasion, in 1989, to ratify the agreement for the Council were, from left to right: Peter Corcoran (Labour), John Hale (Conservative) and Ed Cunniffe (Lib-Dem) and, at the front, Andrew Worthington of Leisure Services.

In November 1989, Tranmere drew Tottenham Hotspur – including Gazza and Gary Lineker – in the Fourth Round of the Littlewoods (League) Cup at Prenton Park. Gascoigne gave Spurs the lead but Steve Vickers (pictured above) levelled the tie and Jim Steel (below) gave Rovers a 2-1 advantage with a flying header, only for poor Dave Higgins to let Spurs of the hook with an own goal and a face-saving replay.

No, the stepladders have not been digitally removed from this April 1990 picture of Steve Mungall, flying high to score a classic header against Preston North End, one of just seventeen goals in 624 appearances for Tranmere.

The Lion of Prenton Park celebrates a rare goal, this time against Brentford in the final League match of the 1989/90 season. Mungall was signed from Motherwell in 1979 and went on to finish his playing career at Prenton Park some sixteen years later – although he is still on the staff in a coaching capacity. Affectionately known as 'Mungy', he was extremely popular with both fans and team mates, who appreciated his total commitment to the cause.

It may only have been a goal against Chester on 6 February 1990, but as far as Ian Muir was concerned it was a record breaker. Goal number 116 of Ian's Tranmere career meant he had overtaken 'Bunny' Bells' fifty-five-year-old club record of League and cup goals. He finished his Rovers career with 180 goals (142 of them in the League) and remains the club's record goalscorer.

In 1989, Tranmere opened their own purpose-built training complex in Valley Road, North Birkenhead. The players' dining room is perhaps one of the last remaining bastions of privacy in a world of media intrusion, but this rare photograph captures players enjoying the traditional beans on toast, tuna salads and pasta.

In 1990, Rovers battled their way through to the Leyland DAF Cup Final at Wembley against Division Three Champions Bristol Rovers – the first of successive visits inside seven days to the twin towers. With a wonderful, hooked volley, Rovers took the lead through Ian Muir, but Bristol levelled through Devon White...

...Cometh the moment, cometh the man! Ian Muir won the ball inside the Bristol penalty area and crossed to the far post where Jim Steel rose above Geoff Twentyman to head powerfully past Parkin, for what proved to be the Tranmere winner.

Harvey's cream! Tranmere captain, Jim Harvey, comes down the steps at Wembley after lifting the Leyland DAF Cup. Eric Nixon, behind him, looks pretty pleased too! Bought in 1987, Harvey was an inspirational leader on the park who was worth every penny of his £25,000 fee.

Over 20,000 Tranmere fans shared the players' joy as they celebrated the sweet taste of Wembley success at the final whistle – sadly a week later it would be the bitter taste of defeat when Notts County overturned Rovers 2-0 in the Third Division Play-off Final.

The 'Goalden' boys – goalscorers Jim Steel and Ian Muir, who enjoyed a highly productive partnership, savour the moment following the presentation. John King said of Steel, 'He's like a maypole, all the others dance around him!'

Well-in-excess of 50,000 people lined the streets of Birkenhead as the team toured the town in an open-topped bus, before arriving at Prenton Park to wild celebrations. Birkenhead had seen nothing like it for fifty-two years.

The fruits of success! John King, the Leyland DAF Cup and the backroom boys who helped lay the foundations for the most successful period in the club's history. From left to right: Ray Mathias (Reserve Team Manager), Ronnie Moore (First Team Coach), John King, Kenny Jones (Trainer) and Warwick Rimmer (Youth Development Officer).

The papers called it 'Unhampered Success' – a reference to the chairman, Peter Johnson's, business empire, Park Hampers. Birkenhead born and bred, Johnson had watched Rovers as a boy in the 1950s, before eventually rescuing the club in 1987. Along with his vice-chairman, Frank Corfe, almost everything they touched turned to gold. One wonders what Tranmere Rovers could have achieved, had Johnson not moved to Everton. A large employer in Birkenhead, Peter Johnson started his multi-million pound public limited company in the rear of his father's butchers shop.

The famous Steve Cooper back flip was only ever seen at Prenton Park once – against Bury on 11 May 1991, when he netted the only home goal of his six for Rovers. A £100,000 buy from Barnsley, Cooper was an accomplished gymnast in his teenage days and became famous for his extravagant, celebratory back-somersaults after scoring.

Apart from reaching the 1990/91 Division Three Play-off Final at Wembley, Rovers also booked a defence of their Leyland DAF Cup against Birmingham, following a 4-1 (on aggregate) defeat of Preston North End in the Northern Final. Here, the players are pictured at Deepdale following the final whistle.

Tranmere fans pose for the camera on Wembley Way, in front of the famous twin towers, before the 1991 Leyland DAF Cup Final with Birmingham City. After three previous visits inside fourteen months, some of the fans were on first name terms with the Wembley stewards!

Trailing to two goals from Simon Sturridge and John Gayle, Rovers staged a remarkable comeback to level the 1991 Leyland DAF Cup Final, firstly from Brummie Steve Cooper (above) and then Jim Steel (below), who wiped out Birmingham's advantage with a towering header. But, with Rovers set for extra time, big John Gayle scored a brilliant winner in the eighty-fourth minute to give the St Andrews outfit the cup. Many regarded it as a blessing in disguise, as it would fire up Rovers for the clash that mattered most – Bolton, the following week.

A ticket to the Promised Land! Chris Malkin hammers in the extra-time goal that broke Bolton hearts and took Tranmere back to Division Two for the first time in fifty-two years. Even referee Keith Hackett seems pleased!

There's no feeling in the world like being a winner at Wembley – particularly when your club has just been promoted. John Morrissey yells with joy at the final whistle.

Above: Captain Eric Nixon, who had taken over as skipper from Jimmy Harvey, raises aloft the League's commemorative pennant in the Royal Box at Wembley on 1 June 1991. *Below*: The whole squad adopts the traditional Wembley winners stance – except that the trophy and the scorer of the winning goal are missing!

Goal-scoring hero Chris Malkin – a former bank worker plucked out of non-League soccer – salutes Tranmere's success, along with the architect of the club's amazing revival, John King. Around the old stadium, jubilant Rovers fans chanted incessantly 'We are going up, say we are going up!' Peter Johnson's promise of Division Two football inside five years was achieved a year early.

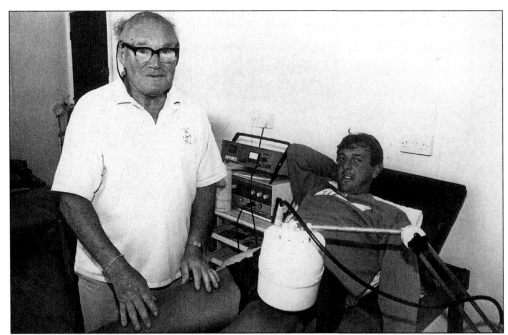

Rovers' promotion was all the more remarkable because it was achieved without the services of their record goal scorer, Ian Muir, who was recovering from a cruciate ligament injury sustained at Macclesfield (Chester's borrowed ground at the time), in March 1991. His recovery was supervised by Alec McLellan, the long-serving physiotherapist.

As part of their grand masterplan, Peter Johnson and John King entrusted the future development of young players to Warwick Rimmer and he set up a School of Excellence for ten to sixteen-year-olds. Here, John King is giving the boys a pep talk as coach John Conroy listens.

In June 1991, Rovers broke their transfer record to bring John Aldridge back to Merseyside from Real Sociedad for £250,000. In his first home game, pre-season, he left his former Liverpool team mates red-faced with Rovers' winner in a 1-0 success.

John Aldridge and Ian Muir celebrate, as 'Aldo' helps Rovers to an incredible 4-3 victory over Derby County in March 1992, in which Tranmere were 3-1 down at one stage.

In November 1992, Rovers embarked on their first-ever European adventure, playing AC Reggiana in the Anglo-Italian Cup. Outside the team's hotel, John King enjoys the autumn sunshine with ninety-two-year-old Rovers fan Margaret McGinlay of Birkenhead.

Peggy Moore worked for Tranmere Rovers for forty-three years, eight of them cooking lunchtime meals for the players at Valley Road Training Ground. Her story even found a spot in Tom Watts' book, *A Passion for the Game*.

'Sometimes in football you get lucky', said John King, who gambled a £10,000 fee on Ian Nolan from non-League Marine. Nolan went on to make the left-back spot his own before being transferred to Sheffield Wednesday in August 1994 for £1,500,000! Nolan subsequently played international football for Northern Ireland, but is pictured here signing for Rovers in August 1991.

Goodison Park was the venue for Rovers 1992 victory in the Liverpool Senior Cup, when they defeated Marine 4-1 to lift the famous old trophy, with a mixture of first team and reserves.

Go for Goal was an instantly forgettable game show screened by Granada TV. Tranmere's team included Chris Malkin and Steve Mungall, along with the captain, Stan Boardman. For the record, they beat Bolton 5-0!

Scottish international winger Pat Nevin became a huge favourite at Prenton Park in the 1990s. Initially signed on loan, his move from Everton was made permanent in August 1992, in exchange for a £300,000 fee. Later becoming the chairman of the PFA, Pat was a great ambassador for Tranmere – both on and off the field – winning fourteen Scottish caps between 1992 and 1996. Though he'd just missed a sitter in this picture, his scoring record at Prenton Park was more than respectable for a winger.

A man and his tractor! Head groundsman Andy Quayle surveys his pitch in 1994, just prior to the start of ground redevelopment. Within months, the old Cowshed and Borough Road stands were demolished and a new pitch laid.

Long-serving club secretary, Norman Wilson, at his desk inside the Valley Road Training Complex. A loyal servant for some twenty-eight years (which included nineteen as secretary, in two spells) he was offered a seat on the board in 1995 and finally retired as secretary two years later, having selected his successor, Mick Horton.

In 1993/94 season, Tranmere reached the Coca Cola Cup Semi-final, and, against all the odds, took a first leg 3-1 lead against Aston Villa at Prenton Park. Attacking full-back Ian Nolan opened the scoring on that memorable night and Mark Hughes cracked in a second.

When John Aldridge made it 3-0, it seemed that Rovers were Wembley-bound again, but Mark Bosnich, on the floor as Aldo scores, was to have the final say in the second leg – which Rovers lost on penalties, after squandering their first leg advantage to leave the score balanced at 4-4.

Where the Germans failed in 1942, Tarmac Construction succeeded in 1994, levelling Prenton Park inside the first two weeks of June. Borough Road was first to fall followed by The Cowshed. Meanwhile, The Paddock was dug up to allow seating to be installed, and a new pitch was laid in just three weeks.

The new, 5,842-seater Kop Stand rises like a phoenix from the ashes. Built inside thirty-eight weeks, the sixty-four-metre long, thirty-six-metre wide and twenty-three-metre high structure unfolded before the eyes of incredulous Rovers fans during the 1994/95 season. Since the Kop was opened in March 1995, the empty spaces underneath have been utilised to create a new training and office complex, to replace Valley Road, which was needed for an industrial estate relief road.

It took only thirteen weeks to transform the Borough Road side into a 2,434-seater stand, which was ready for the first home match of 1994/95 season against Swindon Town. The new Cowshed stand, seating 2,507, was opened before the cup tie with Norwich in late October 1994 and the whole project was completed and officially opened, amid a host of special events, on 11 March 1995, when Grimsby were the visitors. Prenton Park was transformed into a 16,789 all-seater stadium at a cost of £3,100,000 (£2.15 million of which was paid by grants from the Football Trust). The whole scheme was conceived by chairman Frank Corfe, after seeing how Notts County had rebuilt their ground.

A parade of former players were amongst the celebrations on 11 March 1995, when the rebuilt ground was officially opened. From left to right: George Yardley, Mark Palios, Percy Steele, Ralph Millington, Eric Hornby, Dave Hickson, Harold Atkinson, Roy Parnell, Harry Leyland, Joey Pritchard, and Alan King.

The boy pictured earlier in the book (see page 95) with his dad has now grown up! Ian Moore receives his England youth cap from Frank Corfe in November 1995. The young striker subsequently won England under-21 honours before his £1,000,000 transfer to Nottingham Forest in March 1997. Destined to become a footballer ever since he could walk, Ian used to train with the first team during holidays – when he was just thirteen years old! In his sixty-six appearances for Rovers, Ian scored thirteen goals.

The 1997/98 squad line up for the camera, with the influence of John Aldridge now evident. Since taking over from John King in April 1996, Aldridge has wheeled and dealed to re-shape the side. In this picture, Mauro, Andy Parkinson, Andy Thompson, Ryan Williams, Lee Jones, David Kelly and Andy Thorn represent the new era.

John Aldridge signs off as a player with an emotional lap of the ground, following his final appearance against Wolves on 3 May 1998. Now simply manager, Aldo's final tally for Rovers was 174 goals (including two in his final match) in just 294 appearances. Overall, during a brilliant, success-laden career, he scored 474 goals and his final appearance, at thirty-nine years and 227 days, made him the oldest player to appear for Rovers in a League match.

Printed in Great Britain
by Amazon

10088440R00075